D1351202

Hi there Power Rangers fans and welcome to our very own official Power Rangers Annual.

We're Rocky, Kimberly, Adam, Aisha, Billy and Tommy otherwise known to all of you as

and we've taken a little time away from fighting Lord Zedd and his evil minions to fill this book with everything you've ever wanted to know about us.

There are zillions of great photos of our adventures and all the secrets of our incredible powers, as well as some brain-teasing puzzles for you to solve.

Zordon is calling us now so we've got to run, but we hope you enjoy reading all about us in this book.

See you next year!

GO! GO! POWER RANGERS

CONTENTS

Mighty Morphin Power Rangers TM and © 1995 Saban Entertainment, Inc. & Saban International N.V.
All Rights Reserved. SABAN'S MIGHTY MORPHIN POWER RANGERS and all logos, character names and distinctive likenesses thereof are trademarks of Saban Entertainment, Inc. and Saban International N.V.

Licensed by E.C. Licensing Limited

Written and Designed by Century 22 Limited

Published in Great Britain in 1995 by World International, an imprint of Egmont Publishing Ltd, Egmont House, P.O. Box 111, Great Ducie Street, Manchester M60 3BL. Printed in Great Britain ISBN 0 7498 2504 9

THE STORY SO FAR

Evil took the form of the Evil Empress Rita Repulsa, a vile and wretched being who plumbed the very depths of wickedness and savagery in her quest to dominate the universe. She was a scheming, double-dealing and vicious tyrant who would stop at absolutely nothing to achieve her dastardly ends.

Zillions and zillions of years ago, deep in the mists of time a war was being waged across the vastnesses of the universe between the forces of good and evil.

Good was represented by Zordon, an ancient wizard, scholar and sage, who used the profound depths of his humanity and wisdom to fight for what was right.

For thousands upon thousands of years the battle raged as first Zordon and Rita gained the upper hand. Moons, planets and even stars were destroyed by the fearful powers unleashed in the fight. The universe was ravaged by the scars of interstellar war but all to no avail as Zordon and Rita came to realize that they were at a stalemate - they were as powerful as each other and neither could win.

As luck would have it, the dumpster crash-landed on a grey moon orbiting a blue and green planet called Earth. Even this wouldn't have been so bad, but a few thousand years later, two Lunar explorers - or astronauts - found the dumpster and unwittingly set Rita free from her prison.

Zordon had thought of this eventuality and had set up a special, secret Command Centre on Earth. It was manned - if that is the word - by Alpha Five, a cute droid who reported back to his master the moment he detected that Rita had escaped.

Zordon took the initiative and suggested to his adversary that they should toss a coin to see who should rule the universe forever. The wise old wizard won the toss, but the scheming Rita insisted on making it the best of five! Despite his better judgement, Zordon acceded to her wishes and the coin was tossed four more times. It didn't do Rita any good however and Zordon had to decide what to do with her. As so often is the case with the good and the fair-minded, he couldn't bring himself to harm Rita, so instead he imprisoned her with her henchmen in a space dumpster and cast the craft adrift in the depths of interstellar space.

That was the moment that the lives of five young people in nearby Angel Grove were to be changed forever. Zordon told Alpha Five to seek out the best means for combatting Rita. After detailed research through the history of the planet, the droid advised his master that the strongest powers ever to have existed on Earth were dinosaurs and teenagers with attitude!

Frustrated beyond belief as her efforts were thwarted at every turn, the Evil Empress devised a devious plan against the Power Rangers. She used the Power Coin that she had acquired by underhanded means more than 10,000 years ago, to change a local teenager called Tommy into the evil Green Ranger.

Rita used him in her fight against the Power Rangers, but Tommy was not really bad. He fought with all his determination and strength to free himself from Rita's chains of evil. With the help of Jason, who destroyed the sword of darkness, he finally prevailed and Rita's evil spell was broken. Tommy then became the sixth Ranger defending the Earth from terror.

In no time Jason, Trini, Billy, Zack and Kimberly were chosen from the cream of American youth to be the Red, Yellow, Blue, Black and Pink Power Rangers and their powers linked to the mightiest of the dinosaurs. Surprised at first - well, wouldn't you be? - they soon warmed to their task and brought their own individual skills to the fight against Rita.

She threw everything she could at them - monsters of all shapes and sizes and, of course, the Putty Patrol - but while she could sometimes gain a temporary advantage, the Power Rangers, with their Power Coins and Power Zords to help them, always managed to come out on top.

In her fury, Rita and her henchmen began ever more frequent and powerful attacks against the Rangers. Eventually, Rita's wicked and twisted mind came up with a plan to rid herself of the Green Ranger. By attaching a green candle to Tommy's powers, Rita almost captured control of the Dragon Dagger and Dragon Zord.

Tommy proved himself a real hero as, with true grit and determination, he fought Rita and then gave up his powers to Jason rather than lose them to Rita. With Tommy out of the picture, his Zord continued to be used by Jason and the other Rangers as they carried on the fight against the evil cloud over the Earth.

Lord Zedd, from a far away solar system, decided that Rita had not utilized all her powers well enough to fight the Power Rangers. Resolving to replace her himself, he placed her in a dumpster and flung her out to float in space.

The Power Rangers soon felt the force of his increased powers as he destroyed all of their Zords, leaving the Power Rangers helpless. With fragments of the old Zords the ingenious Alpha Five was able to build stronger and more powerful Thunderzords - the Unicorn, Tiger, Dragon, Lion, Griffin and Firebird. Feeling the increasing rage of evil on Earth, Zordon and Alpha Five worked to construct a new sixth Ranger. Zordon felt that Tommy had proved himself to be worthy, courageous and truthful and so he chose him to be the newly created White Ranger. Tommy's powers were derived from the light of goodness and can therefore never be taken away by evil forces.

Now with the help of his powerful White Tigerzord and mightily talking Saber Sword, Saba, Tommy and the other Power Rangers are ready to take on Lord Zedd's monsters.

Go! Go! Power Rangers!!

TOMMY

THE GREEN & WHITE RANGER

The most sensitive, of the Power Rangers, Tommy was the sixth teenager from Angel Grove to join the team of superheroes as the Green Ranger.

He had a nefarious beginning to his career, however, as he was originally kidnapped by Rita Repulsa and forced to infiltrate the Power Rangers and defeat them for the forces of Evil. Under the Empress of Evil's control, Tommy penetrated the command centre and destroyed Alpha Five's circuits with a computer virus. As Tommy switched off Zordon's communication devices, Alpha Five managed to capture Tommy

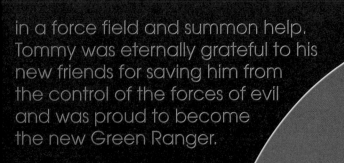

in a force field and summon help. Tommy was eternally grateful to his new friends for saving him from the control of the forces of evil and was proud to become the new Green Ranger.

He had been a bit of a loner ever since he was a child and was glad to be part of a team. He brought his invaluable skills as an accomplished black belt karate martial artist to the Power Rangers and is a ferocious opponent for Lord Zedd and his minions.

The Green Ranger's powers had originated from the dark side and so inevitably soon began to fail. His Dragon Dagger lost its powers and his Dragonzord returned to the sea, leaving him out of commission and unable to help his friends in their fight against Lord Zedd. He started to have nightmares about his plight and almost fell into Goldar's clutches, nearly losing the Sword of Power at the same time. He fought bravely against Robogoat and Guitardo but then, collapsing from near exhaustion, he was captured by the Turban Shell monster.

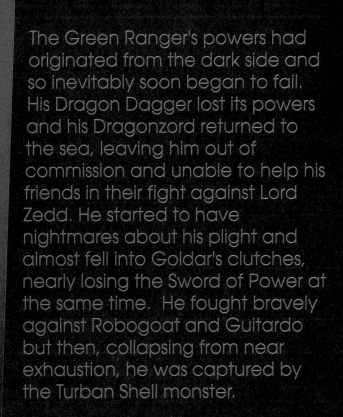

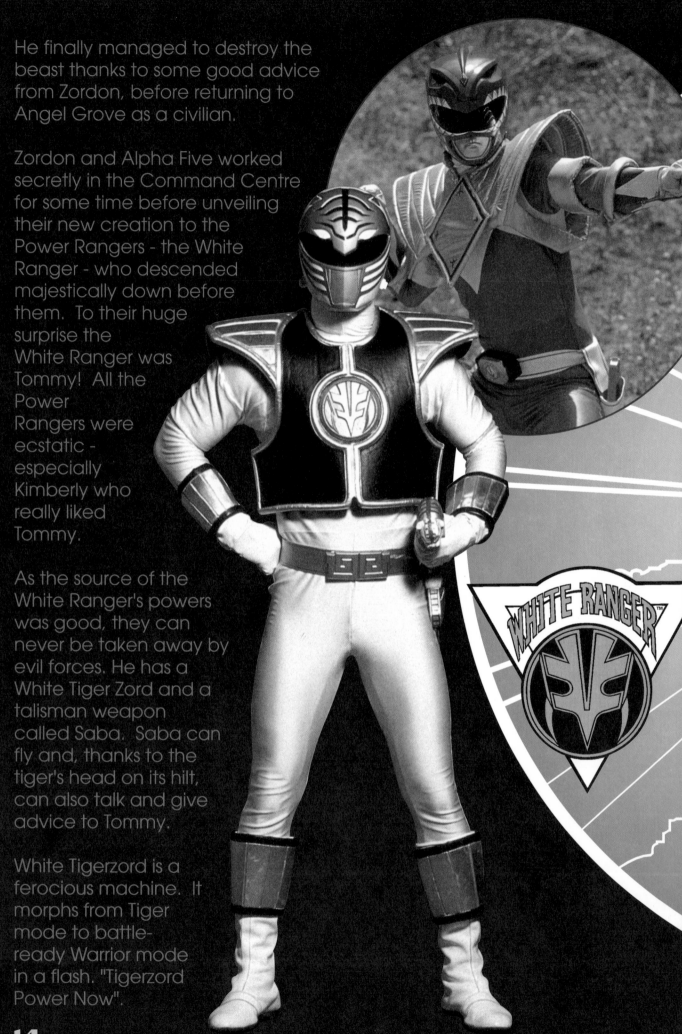

He finally managed to destroy the beast thanks to some good advice from Zordon, before returning to Angel Grove as a civilian.

Zordon and Alpha Five worked secretly in the Command Centre for some time before unveiling their new creation to the Power Rangers - the White Ranger - who descended majestically down before them. To their huge surprise the White Ranger was Tommy! All the Power Rangers were ecstatic - especially Kimberly who really liked Tommy.

As the source of the White Ranger's powers was good, they can never be taken away by evil forces. He has a White Tiger Zord and a talisman weapon called Saba. Saba can fly and, thanks to the tiger's head on its hilt, can also talk and give advice to Tommy.

White Tigerzord is a ferocious machine. It morphs from Tiger mode to battle-ready Warrior mode in a flash. "Tigerzord Power Now".

WHITE RANGER™

Colour: Green, White

Weapon: Dragon Dagger, Saba

Power Source: Dragon, Tiger

Vehicle: Dragonzord,
White Tigerzord

WHITE TIGERZORD RED DRAGON THUNDERZORD AND UNICORN THUNDERZORD

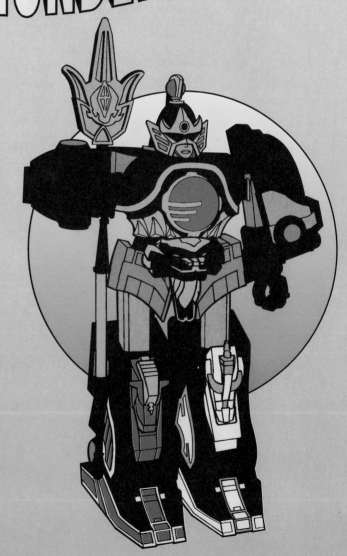

These three amazing Thunderzords are the new zords belonging to the White, Red and Blue Rangers. After their old Dinozords - Dragonzord, Tyrannosaurus Dinozord and Triceratops Dinozord - were rendered useless by the bolt fired by Lord Zedd, which blocked their controls, Zordon created these fearsome new Thunderzords for his Power Rangers. Armed with their new powers, they pose an even greater threat to the evil space aliens and can defend the Earth better than ever before.

Together with the Lion, Griffin and Firebird Thunderzords they can morph into the awesome Mega Thunderzord, which can defeat anything that Lord Zedd can throw against it.

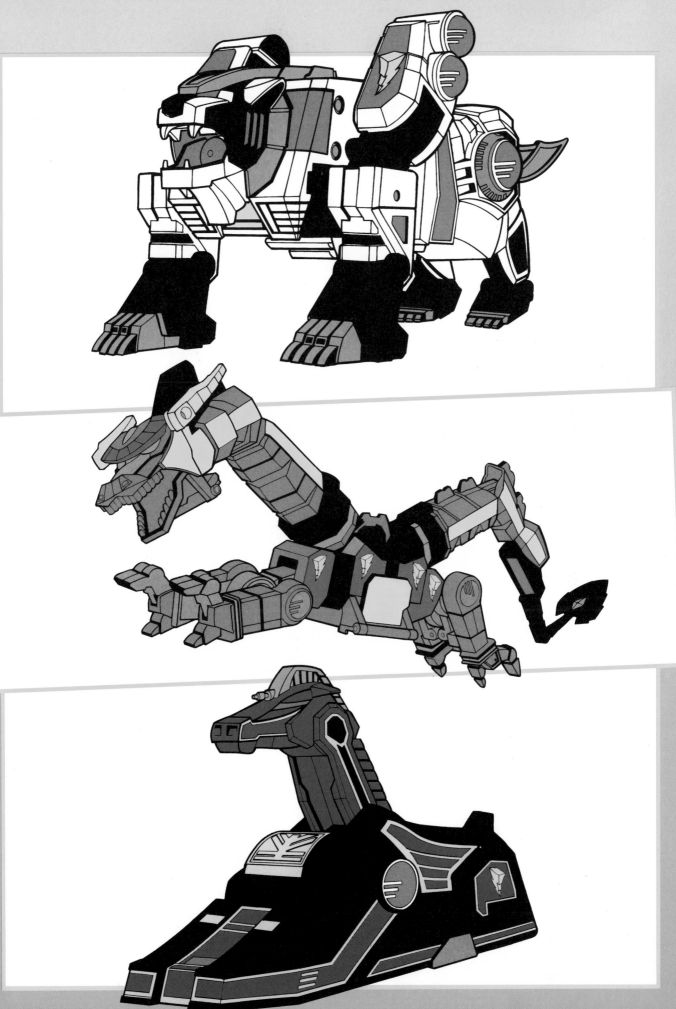

JASON & ROCKY

THE RED RANGER

Right from the start, Jason was the Red Ranger and the undisputed leader of the Power Rangers. Like Tommy, he had spent years studying karate and attained the highest levels of skill before being awarded his black belt. He spends a lot of his spare time on honing his martial art skills as well as learning new ones.

At school, Jason is just like any other teenager. He is full of the hopes and dreams of the young for the future of the world. A hard working student, he can also be playful - his mischievous streak often comes to the surface to both the surprise and amusement of his friends.

Always friendly and cheerful, Jason can be rather introverted, often preferring to keep his feelings to himself. But whenever the forces of evil are on the march, they soon feel what Jason has to say - through the well-aimed punches and kicks which do his talking for him.

Ever courageous, Jason played a major part in rescuing Tommy from Goldar and one of Lord Zedd's evil monsters Robogoat, after Goldar had drained his friend's powers and stolen the Sword of Power. In a fantastic fighting display the Red Ranger managed to knock the

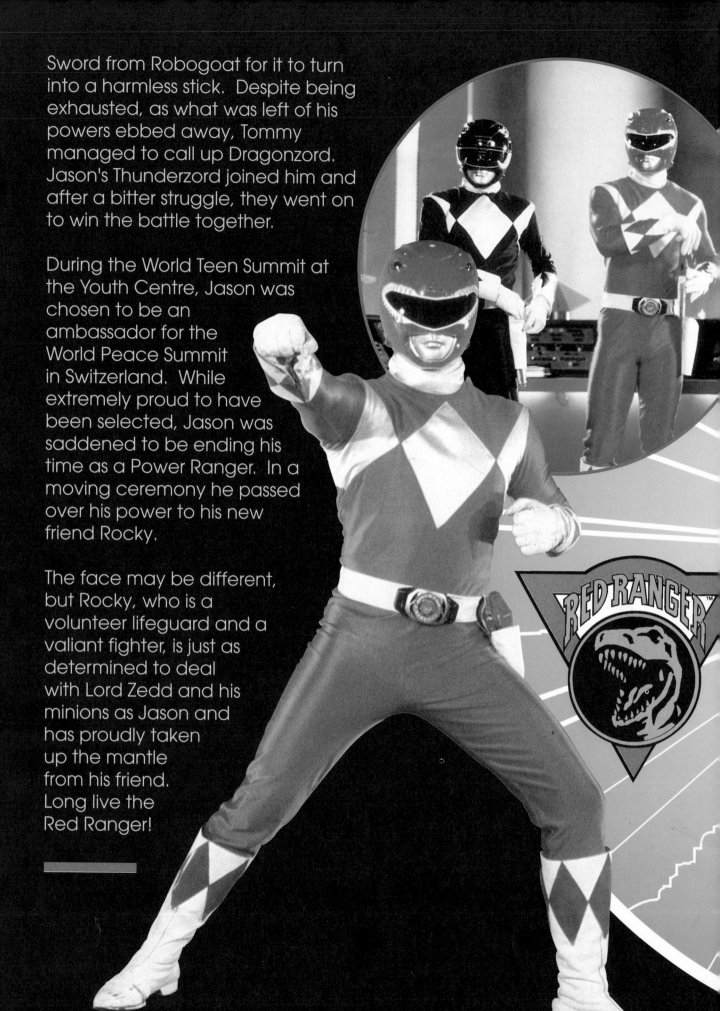

Sword from Robogoat for it to turn into a harmless stick. Despite being exhausted, as what was left of his powers ebbed away, Tommy managed to call up Dragonzord. Jason's Thunderzord joined him and after a bitter struggle, they went on to win the battle together.

During the World Teen Summit at the Youth Centre, Jason was chosen to be an ambassador for the World Peace Summit in Switzerland. While extremely proud to have been selected, Jason was saddened to be ending his time as a Power Ranger. In a moving ceremony he passed over his power to his new friend Rocky.

The face may be different, but Rocky, who is a volunteer lifeguard and a valiant fighter, is just as determined to deal with Lord Zedd and his minions as Jason and has proudly taken up the mantle from his friend. Long live the Red Ranger!

RED RANGER™

Colour:	**Red**
Weapon:	**Power Sword**
Power Source:	**Tyrannosaurus Rex**
Vehicle:	**Red Dragon Thunderzord**

LORD ZEDD'S MONSTERS

INCLUDING RITA'S NASTY CREATIONS

Ever since Lord Zedd and Rita turned their evil eye on the Earth, they have revelled in sending ever more bizarre and fiendish monsters to combat Zordon and his Power Rangers.

Our heroic team of teenagers with attitude have had to fight a never-ending series of ne'er-do-wells created from an incredible variety of sources. Lord Zedd and Rita uses their evil magic to create monsters from creatures and objects found on Earth. These range from the Giant Hen who is equipped with two pairs of shears, Primator who was transformed from Billy's gorilla suit to Purselips who started life as Kimberly's purse!

While they can all be troublesome customers, Zordon and his friends are always a match for their evil intentions.

BILLY

THE BLUE RANGER

Behind the mask of the Blue Ranger you can find the most ultra-intelligent kid in Angel Grove. Billy is really a super genius whose whole life revolves around computers, science and - best of all - inventing crazy, and sometimes, extraordinary devices.

When he speaks, you sometimes need an interpreter to understand what he is saying because Billy often talks his own special techno-speak. Every sentence seems to be peppered with scientific terms and technical jargon.

Tending towards being rather shy and quiet, Billy is really a sweet and good-hearted guy who can always be relied on to get his friends out of a tight corner. He always thinks every problem through, looking at it from every angle before tackling it. This thoroughness, together with his acute intelligence, usually leads to Billy resolving just about any problem he faces and coming out on top.

Trini is the only one of the Power Rangers who can really understand what Billy says, but of course Alpha Five is totally tuned into Billy's thought patterns. They are often to be found together working on ingenious new machines to thwart the evil Lord Zedd's plans.

At school and when not in class, Billy can usually be found in the computer centre, testing a new scientific theory or working on a new invention. He is a great joiner of clubs such as the Maths Club, the Chess Club, the Science Club, the Debate Team and, of course, MENSA.

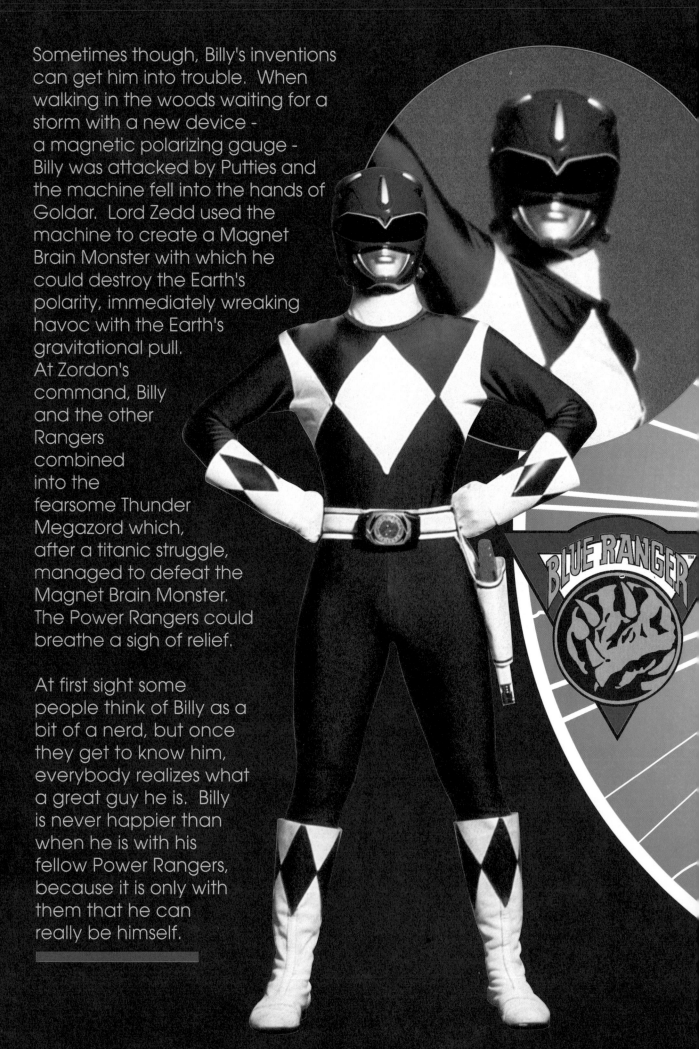

Sometimes though, Billy's inventions can get him into trouble. When walking in the woods waiting for a storm with a new device - a magnetic polarizing gauge - Billy was attacked by Putties and the machine fell into the hands of Goldar. Lord Zedd used the machine to create a Magnet Brain Monster with which he could destroy the Earth's polarity, immediately wreaking havoc with the Earth's gravitational pull. At Zordon's command, Billy and the other Rangers combined into the fearsome Thunder Megazord which, after a titanic struggle, managed to defeat the Magnet Brain Monster. The Power Rangers could breathe a sigh of relief.

At first sight some people think of Billy as a bit of a nerd, but once they get to know him, everybody realizes what a great guy he is. Billy is never happier than when he is with his fellow Power Rangers, because it is only with them that he can really be himself.

BLUE RANGER

Colour:	**Blue**
Weapon:	**Power Lance**
Power Source:	**Triceratops**
Vehicle:	**Unicorn Thunderzord**

THE PUTTY PATROL

When Rita Repulsa first commanded Finster to create a legion of footsoldiers to aid her quest to conquer the Earth, he turned to an incredibly ordinary natural substance - clay.

In just a few seconds, he can transform a simple grey lump in one of his fiendish moulds into a mindless, but all-action, fighting member of the Putty Patrol.

Always ready to ambush the Power Rangers, these creatures aren't blessed with too much intelligence and can be destroyed by a karate kick to the 'Z' badge worn on their chest.

BULK & SKULL

These clumsy oafs are the outcasts of Angel Grove. Always scheming and trying to outwit the more popular members of Angel Grove High, their plans always seem to fall apart at the seams.

Whenever they try to outwit Rocky, Kimberly, Adam, Aisha, Tommy and Billy they always end up with the short end of the stick. They love to play practical jokes, but it is always them that ends up covered in slime or falling in the pond!

Bulk is the larger of the two and you can see why. Wherever he goes, there is always food near at hand - and preferably loads and loads of it! Skull thinks he's really cool and his main trademark - apart from a lack of brains - is that he is always chewing gum. Those jaws are going to stick together one day!

An unlikely, incompetent, blundering and bungling pair, they are determined to discover the secret identity of the Power Rangers. Secretly, though, they would like nothing better than to join them. Can you really imagine Bulk and Skull as superheroes?

THE POWER RANGERS AT BATTLE STATIONS

Here are the team at battle stations against yet another bunch evil monsters and nasty putties. It's going to be a fight to the finish, but our super heroes are sure to end up on top.

POWER RANGERS MEGA QUIZ

How much do you really know about the Power Rangers and their world?
Test out your knowledge on this Mega Quiz and see if you know enough to become a Power Ranger yourself!

1. What does Skull always seem to have in his mouth?

2. Kimberly is very fashion conscious. What does she love to do in the Valley malls?

3. Who would you find at the controls of the Griffin Thunderzord

4. What is the Red Ranger's weapon called?

5. What does Finster use to make the Putties?

6. Which dinosaur gives Kimberly her special powers?

7. In what was Rita Repulsa confined by Zordon and sent spinning through eternity?

8. Who uses the Power Lance in the fight against Lord Zedd?

9. Who pilots the Tyrannosaurus Zord?

10. What is the Carrier Zord called?

11. Who would you find at the controls of the Mastodon Zord?

12. What is Rita Repulsa's motto?

13. Which Ranger uses the Power Bow?

14. Which dinosaur gives Trini her special powers?

15. How old was Tommy when he fell under the spell of Rita Repulsa?

16. Which Ranger uses the Dragon Dagger?

17. What was the monster called that Lord Zedd created out of a piranha fish?

18. Which Ranger is a member of MENSA?

19. Which dinosaur gives Jason his special powers?

20. Who did Goldar kidnap and take to Venus Island, home of the Invenusable Fly Trap?

21. What did Tommy and Kimberly combine to defeat Guitardo?

22. Which dinosaur gives Billy his special powers?

23. Lord Zedd recruited a team of teenagers to fight the Power Rangers. What were they called?

24. Goldar kidnapped Kimberly when she visited a gypsy fortune teller for information about Tommy. What was she called?

25. What did Lord Zedd use to create the Scarlet Sentinel monster?

26. Which dinosaur gives Zack his special powers?

27. Who were the winners of the Ninja Competition?

28. Zack, Trini and Jason were ambassadors to the World Peace Conference. Where was it to be held?

29. From what powerful animal does Tommy derive his special powers?

30. What good work does Rocky do in his spare time?

Find out the answers on page 60

35

LION, GRIFFIN AND FIREBIRD THUNDERZORDS

When Lord Zedd unleashed his fury on the Dinozords he fired a bolt which jammed their controls forever. The Dinozords belonging to the Black, Yellow and Pink Rangers - Mastodon Dinozord, Sabre-tooth Tiger Dinozord and Pterodactyl Dinozord - were now completely useless, so Zordon and Alpha Five decided to create newer, even more powerful Thunderzords for their protegés.

So were born the Lion, Griffin and Firebird Thunderzords which give their owners phenomenal powers of strength, resilience and firepower to help them in their struggle against Lord Zedd and his evil minions.

Together with the White Lion, Red Dragon and Unicorn Thunderzords they can morph into the awesome Mega Thunderzord, which can defeat anything that Lord Zedd can throw against it.

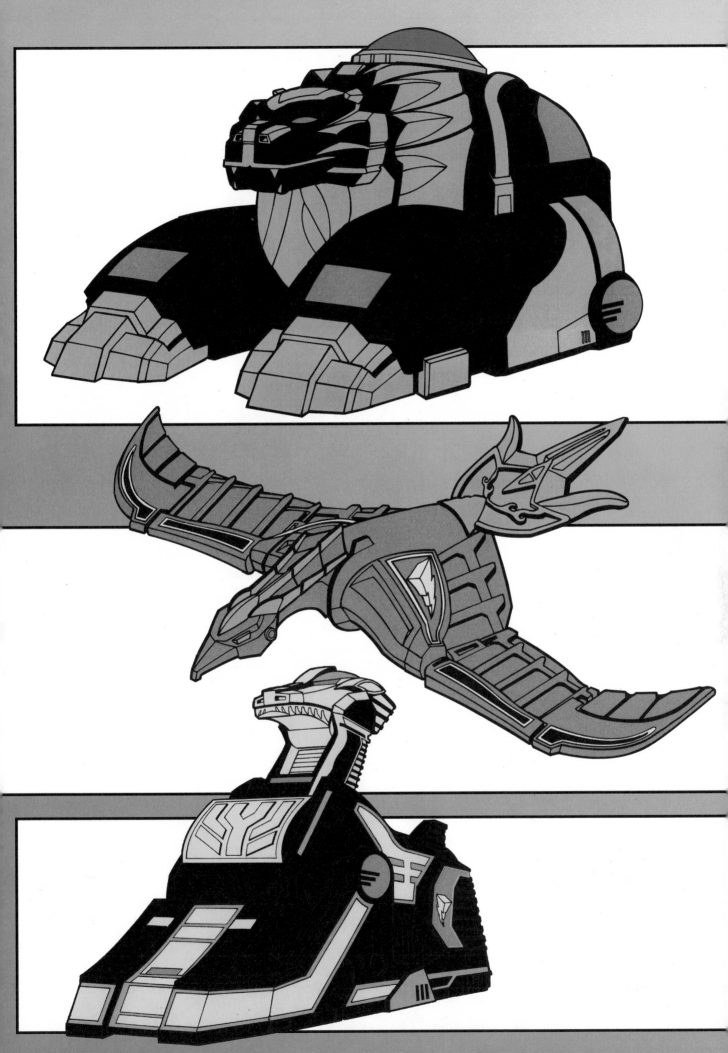

KIMBERLY

THE PINK RANGER

The Pink Ranger is a popular girl who has plenty of brains behind her pretty face. That's not to say that, like most of her teenage school pals, she is not interested in fashion though. Kimberly is happiest when she is out shopping for clothes, jewellery and make up in the Angel Grove shopping mall. But she is no spoiled "valley" rat, shopping is just her way of being nice to herself.

Apart from looking good, Kimberly's other great passion in life is gymnastics. She has put years of practice into her sport and has developed her natural talent to the highest level, becoming a champion gymnast. This talent comes in very handy for her other role as a Power Ranger.

Her years of training in the gym have given her a supple and powerful physique which are great qualities to have in battle. She is especially effective when Putties are around. Being so athletic and nimble she literally back flips rings round Lord Zedd's creations before destroying them with ease.

Kimberly has a playful nature and is always ready for a laugh or prank. She is always sweet with her friends though - especially Tommy - saving her ready wit and sarcasm for the bad guys.

She has had some close calls in her career as a Power Ranger. None more so than when she decided to visit a gypsy fortune teller to try and get some information about Tommy. As Madame Swampy looked into her crystal ball, Goldar threw dust over Kimberly and kidnapped her. Lord Zedd then used Kimberly's mirror to create the Mirror Maniac Monster and transformed the luckless girl into Goldar's queen. When Billy and Zack arrived, they saw that she had been bluffing all along.

They joined with her and the other Power Rangers, summoned their Thunderzords and, with the Thunder Megazord, defeated the Mirror Monster.

Kimberly's strong and independent spirit leads her to long for excitement, adventure and danger and, as a founder member of the Power Rangers, she has seen plenty of all three. She has fought resolutely and victoriously with Jason, Trini, Zack, Billy and Tommy against the worst monsters Lord Zedd could throw at them. ▬▬▬

PINK RANGER™

Colour:	**Pink**
Weapon:	**Power Bow**
Power Source:	**Pterodactyl**
Vehicle:	**Firebird Thunderzord**

LORD ZEDD'S MONSTERS

INCLUDING RITA'S NASTY CREATIONS

The evil Lord Zedd will stop at nothing in his fight against the forces of good in the person of Zordon, Alpha Five and the Power Rangers.

Here are some more of the fiendish creatures who help him fulfil his quest to rule the universe. They all have special powers and strengths, but as they are fed by the power of evil, they will all ultimately fail when fought by the Power Rangers.

When evil forces threaten to overwhelm the Power Rangers they combine their powers to form the mighty, Power Sword-wielding Thunder Megazord - a morphinomenal combination of all the Ranger's Thunderzords.

GO! GO! POWER RANGERS!!

TRINI & AISHA

THE YELLOW RANGER

Trini is another of the original members of the Power Rangers who has found a new and important role in her life as a World Teenage Peace Ambassador. Little did she realize, when the Youth Centre at Angel Grove played host to the World Teen Summit, that she would be chosen, along with her Power Ranger friends Jason and Zack, to be a Teenage Peace Ambassador.

Up until then, her life had been a continual series of action-packed adventures which had started when, as a "teenager with attitude", she was chosen by Zordon to be the Yellow Ranger and help in the fight to save the Earth from the malevolent intentions of Lord Zedd and the Empire of Evil.

A delightfully pretty girl with long, flowing black hair, Trini is a consummate martial artist who can fell a Putty in a flash with her lightning hands. Beneath her fighting skills she hides a peaceful soul and a thoughtful approach to life. Trini is deeply interested in Eastern philosophy and is a quiet girl who keeps herself to herself at school. By contrast she enjoys taking part in school events, although she is not one to push herself forward as a leader.

By nature she is cautious and, like her friend Zack, she likes to consider all options and possibilities before taking a decision. Once committed to a course of action though, she is totally committed and tenacious - no-one can make her deviate from her chosen path. Although slow to anger, once pushed beyond her limit she can defeat the most ignominious of

Lord Zedd's monsters with consummate ease.

Trini first met Aisha at a Ninja competition. Kimberly, Billy and Tommy had already met Aisha and her friends Rocky and Adam in the park when, together, they had helped save a baby in a runaway pram. At the competition the three winners turned out to be Aisha, Rocky and Adam who were unaware that Lord Zedd had decided to capture the winners to serve him. Goldar took them to the Dimension of Despair and the Power Rangers determined to save their new friends.

Despite being distracted by attacks from Terror Blossom and the Hatchosaurus, Billy, Kimberly and Tommy were sent by Zordon to save Aisha, Rocky and Adam from the Serpent of Darkness. At one point in the rescue Billy had to remove his helmet to breathe and so revealed his true identity to Aisha, Rocky and Adam who then took a vow before Zordon never to reveal their secret.

YELLOW RANGER

Colour:	**Yellow**
Weapon:	**Power Dagger**
Power Source:	**Sabre-Tooth Tiger**
Vehicle:	**Griffin Thunderzord**

ZACK & ADAM

THE BLACK RANGER

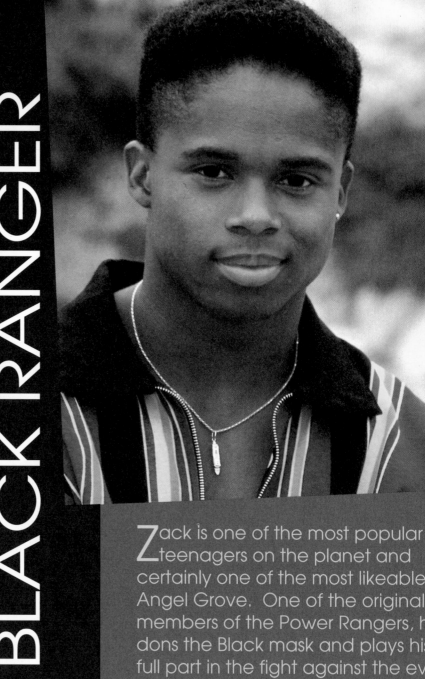

Zack is one of the most popular teenagers on the planet and certainly one of the most likeable in Angel Grove. One of the original members of the Power Rangers, he dons the Black mask and plays his full part in the fight against the evil Lord Zedd and his minions.

His great loves in life are dance and music. A talented and accomplished gymnast, he likes to combine his passions with his skills as a martial artist to form a new style that he calls Hip-Hop-Kiddo.

There is an intelligent and thoughtful brain behind those laughing eyes. He is a great

Drawing his power from the awesome Mastodon that dominated the Earth in prehistory, as the Black Ranger Zack has fought with tenacity and great courage against Lord Zedd and will go to any lengths to thwart his foe's evil ambitions. His weapon is the fearsome Power Axe which he wields with practised skill.

When the World Teen Summit came to the Youth Centre at Angel Grove, Zack was one of the obvious candidates to be chosen to be a Teenage Peace Ambassador. Typically, our

believer in intuition and will always go with his "gut feelings". Indeed, his sensible, cautious nature serves as a great counterbalance to Jason's gung-ho attitude when the Power Rangers are threatened by Lord Zedd's monsters.

Zack seems to be powered by a boundless supply of energy and lights up a room the moment he enters it. Streetwise, smart and a smooth talker, he is the master of the disarming smile and can always use his charm to get his way.

modest hero was genuinely surprised to have been selected, but accepted the honour proudly. His happiness was tinged with sadness however, at the thought of having to leave Tommy, Kimberly and Billy back in Angel Grove. But he knew that his new mission was just as important as the one he was leaving behind. He was thrilled when Zordon announced that the new Black Ranger was to be his new friend Adam. Zack knew that Adam would give Lord Zedd no quarter and that he would fight valiantly for Zordon's cause against the worst that the dark side could throw at him.

BLACK RANGER

Colour:	**Black**
Weapon:	**Power Axe**
Power Source:	**Mastodon**
Vehicle:	**Lion Thunderzord**

WORD TREE

All the words in this list fit into this Power Rangers Word Tree.
Can you get them all into the right places?

ADAM
AISHA
FIREBIRD
GOLDAR
GREEN RANGER
KIMBERLY
LORD ZEDD
MASTODON
POWER COINS
POWER DAGGER
PUTTY PATROL
RED DRAGON
SKULL
TRICERATOPS
ZORDON

The answer is on page 61.

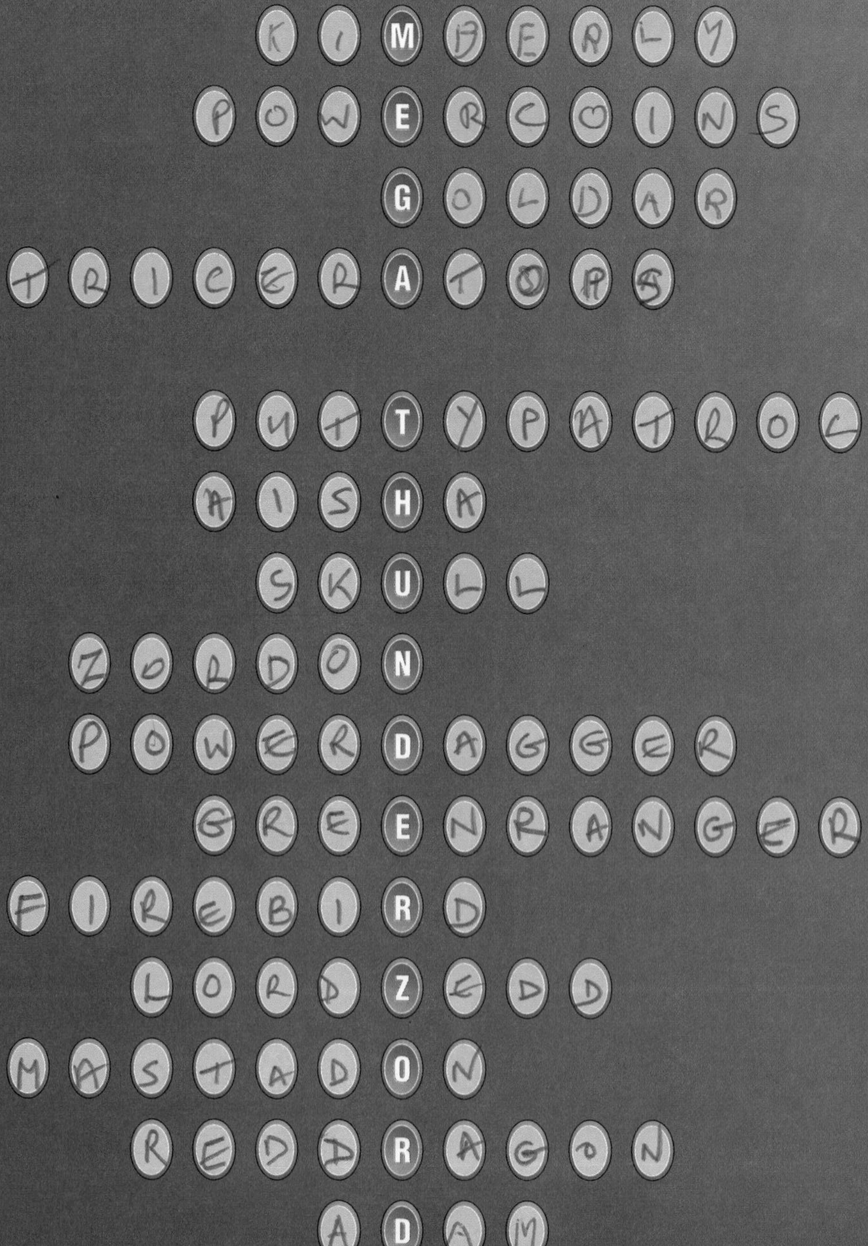

KIMBERLY
POWERCOINS
GOLDAR
TRICERATOPS
PUTTYPATROL
AISHA
SKULL
ZORDON
POWERDAGGER
GREENRANGER
FIREBIRD
LORDZEDD
MASTADON
REDDRAGON
ADAM

MEGA WORDSEARCH

There are 27 Power Rangers words hidden in this Mega Wordsearch. See how many you can hunt down, but remember that the words can go forwards, backwards or diagonally.

Answers on page 61.

BANDAI
COMPETITION

Zordon and Alpha Five have given the Power Rangers the ultimate in weapons to use in their fight with Lord Zedd and his monstrous creations. Here's your chance to win your very own incredible battle team from Bandai the makers of sensational Power Rangers toys.

The lucky First Prize Winner will receive a

Thunder Ultrazord

Which comprises of

The Red Ranger's awesome Red Dragon Thunderzord with the ability to morph from Dragon mode into Warrior mode.

The White Ranger's White Tigerzord that Tommy can summon with Saba, his talking Saber.

Tor - the Power Zord who gets good mileage and gets the job done.

Thunderzord Assault Team which includes the Firebird, Lion, Unicorn and Griffin Thunderzords.

Plus

12 runners-up will each win a Karate Action Power Ranger Figure with special karate action arm movements.

All you have to do to enter is answer the following question:-

What colour is the Power Ranger who commands the Griffin Thunderzord?

Send your entry, stating your full name, address and age to:-

Power Rangers Competition,
Marketing Department
Egmont Publishing
P.O. Box 111
Great Ducie Street
Manchester M60 3BL

Closing Date: 1st February 1996

Rules of Entry

Employees of World International or their respective agents may not enter this competition.

The Editor's decision is final and no correspondence will be entered into.

A list of winners' names will be available on request and on receipt of a SAE after the 14th of February 1996.

The publishers reserve the right to vary the prizes, subject to availability at the time of judging the competition.

THE POWER RANGERS IN ACTION

Rita Repulsa's clumsy attempts to defeat the Power Rangers led to her banishment by the evil Lord Zedd. Now he has an entourage of even more monstrous creatures in tow.

Lord Zedd and his minions have another fight on their hands. Summoning up the primeval forces of the dinosaurs and the enormous power of the Thundorzords the Power Rangers get ready to fight for Zordon and to save the Earth once again.

They use all the powers at their command - strength, agility, martial arts skills and their quick wits to come out on top once more.

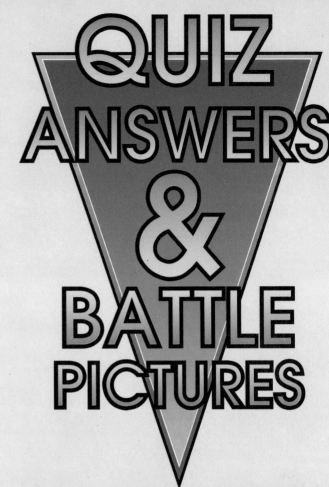

QUIZ ANSWERS & BATTLE PICTURES

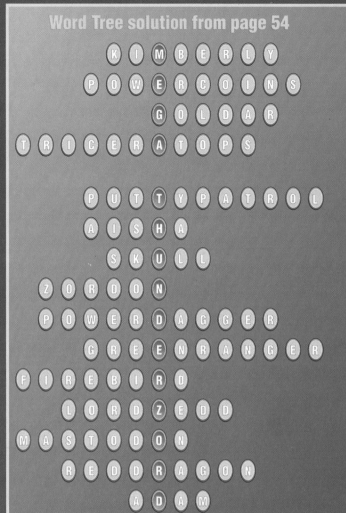

Word Tree solution from page 54

```
        K I M B E R L Y
        P O W E R C O I N S
            G O L D A R
T R I C E R A T O P S
```

```
            P U T T Y P A T R O L
            A I S H A
            S K U L L
        Z O R D O N
        P O W E R D A G G E R
            G R E E N R A N G E R
    F I R E B I R D
        L O R D Z E D D
    M A S T O D O N
            R E D D R A G O N
                A D A M
```

Wordsearch solution from page 55

```
P O W E R R A N G E R S Q X B V
U O Q R N K H Z R K C A Z R O K
T D W R V N I N I R T B I E A L
T R X E D R O J F P O E J G F U
Y Y Y D R O V L F A M R P G J B
P L L D I C G U I D M S R A O D
A L R R B I O L N U Y W S D M R
T I E A E N T I E M C O P N L O
R B B G R U F V N P N R Y O L Z
O T M O I E I P T S S D W G U R
L P I N F F W Q T T S L K A K E
Y N K R A J U I C E B A R R S D
U O L H J T I G E R Z O R D O N
T I P N D E V O R G L E G N A U
P L O R D Z E D D L G T D W P H
A L P H P E K I B R E D N U H T
```